presents

D1461388

salt.

written and performed by
SELINA THOMPSON

salt. premiered at the Southbank Centre, London, in July 2017

salt.

written and performed by Selina Thompson

Directed by	**Dawn Walton**
Designed by	**Katherina Radeva**
Lighting Design	**Cassie Mitchell**
Relights	**Louise Gregory**
Sound Design	**Tanuja Amarasuriya**
Music Composers	**Sleepdogs**
Dramaturgical Support	**Maddy Costa, Season Butler**
Produced by	**Emma Beverley**
Production Manager	**Louise Gregory**

Commissioned by Yorkshire Festival, Theatre Bristol and MAYK. Developed with the National Theatre New Work Department. Supported by Arts Council England and 200 kind and generous supporters who donated towards our voyage across the Atlantic

Winner of *The Stage* Edinburgh Award

Winner of the Total Theatre Award for Experimentation, Innovation and Playing with Form

Winner of the Filipa Bragança Award for Best Female Solo Performance

Shortlisted for the Amnesty International Freedom of Speech Award

www.selinathompson.co.uk

Creative Team

Selina Thompson

is an artist and performer whose work has been shown and praised internationally. Her practice is primarily intimate, political and participatory with a strong emphasis on public engagement that leads to joyous, highly visual work that seeks to connect with those often marginalised by the arts.

Selina's work is focused on the politics of identity, and how this defines our bodies, lives and environments. She has made work for pubs, cafés, hairdressers, toilets, and sometimes even galleries and theatres, including Spill Festival of Performance, the National Theatre Studio, the Birmingham REP, East Street Arts and the West Yorkshire Playhouse, as well as theatres in Europe, Brazil, Canada, the US, and Australia.

Selina has been described as 'a force of nature' (*The Stage*) and 'an inspiration' (*The Independent*). She was featured in *The Stage* 100 Most Influential Leaders 2018, as well as being named in the 'Top Ten Black British Women Killing It in Their Field' (*Buzzfeed*).

Tanuja Amarasuriya

is a Director and Sound Designer who works across theatre, film and digital sound. As a Director and Dramaturg she has worked with playwrights and theatremakers including Timothy X Atack, Dipika Guha, Sam Halmarack, Eno Mfon, Marietta Kirkbride and Raucous.

As Sound Designer, she has worked with Selina Thompson, Chris Thorpe & Rachel Chavkin, and Sookie Greene. She is Co-Artistic Director of *Sleepdogs*, a wide-ranging collaboration with writer and composer Timothy X Atack, making theatre, film and audio work characterised by imaginative storytelling and visceral, emotional, sensory aesthetics. Her work has been developed and presented nationally and internationally, including the National Theatre (London); Bristol Old Vic, New Wolsey Theatre, Seattle International Film Festival, Manchester Royal Exchange, Channel 4 Television, NexT International Film Festival (Bucharest); BIOS (Athens) and Sura Medura (Sri Lanka). She is a Leverhulme Arts Scholar attached to Bristol Old Vic and a resident at Watershed's Pervasive Media Studio.

www.sleepdogs.org

Katherina Radeva

was born in Bulgaria and completed her education in England, training in Design for Performance at Wimbledon School of Art. She was a Linbury Prize for Stage Design finalist in 2005.

Since then she has designed sets and costumes at a variety of scales for stages, outdoor events and site-specific projects. Working mainly with UK companies, her designs have toured globally. Additionally, she has a solo performance practice and has collaborated with other makers to devise work, including as a director of the award-winning *Two Destination Language*.

Key partners as well as Selina Thompson have included Scottish Dance Theatre, Kate Weare, Lost Dog, Trestle Theatre, Horse and Bamboo, the Royal Court Theatre, Andy Manley and Redbridge Arts.

www.katherinaradeva.co.uk
www.twodestinationlanguage.com

Dawn Walton

is Founder and Artistic Director of Eclipse Theatre Company, the UK's principal Black-led national touring company. With over twenty years in the industry, Dawn began her directing career at the Royal Court Theatre. As director and primary artist for Eclipse, Dawn has delivered many productions including *Black Men Walking, A Raisin in the Sun, One Monkey Don't Stop No Show* and *The Hounding of David Oluwale*. Dawn developed and directed the *10by10* short film series of original dramas and *The Last Flag* (BBC Radio 4 Drama). Other recent productions include **salt.** (Selina Thompson Ltd), *Winners, The Blacks* (Young Vic Theatre) and *Lyrikal Fearta* (Sadlers Wells).

Emma Beverley

is an independent producer and programmer based in the UK. She is Selina Thompson's Producer, Executive Producer for Eclipse Theatre Company and founder of The Producer School. She recently worked as Programmer on Leeds' bid to become European Capital of Culture in 2023, and at Homo Novus Festival (Riga, Latvia) to deliver their school for ten international artists. Emma is alumni of the IETM Campus and was supported by the National Theatre throughout 2017 as part of *Step Change.*

Emma has produced and toured work to Canada, the US, Brazil, Australia and across Europe. With Selina Thompson, she has taken work to Canada, the US, Brazil, Australia and across Europe.

Cassie Mitchell

trained in Lighting Design at RADA. Lighting Design credits include: *Angry* (Southwark Playhouse), **salt**. (Bristol Arnolfini and tour), *Opera Scenes* (Guildhall School), *Dark and Lovely* (Ovalhouse), *21,000 Miles of Rail* (UK tour), *Broken Pieces* and *Women of Twilight* (George Bernard Shaw Theatre), *New Labour* (Vanbrugh Theatre).

Assistant Lighting Design includes: *Hamilton* (Victoria Palace Theatre), *School of Rock* (New London Theatre)*, Beautiful: The Carole King Musical* (Aldwych Theatre).

Cassie also works in television on shows such as *Love Island, The Great Pottery Throw Down* and *Strictly Come Dancing.* This autumn she will be the Assistant Lighting Designer for *Come from Away.*

Louise Gregory

works as a Production and Stage Manager, and a Lighting and Sound Designer. For Selina Thompson she has been Production Manager for **salt.**, *Race Cards*, *The Missy Elliott Project* and the forthcoming *Sortition*. Other credits include Production Manager for *The Believers Are but Brothers* with Javaad Alipoor, *The Claim* for Mark Maughan; Production Manager/Set & Costume Designer for *The Siege of Christmas* for Contact Young Company/Slung Low; Company Stage Manager for Scamp Theatre's production of *Stick Man*; Technical Tour Manager for Third Angel's *Partus*; and Technical Manager/Lighting Designer for *Inherited Cities*, also for Third Angel. Recent design credits also include Sound Designer for *Blackout* for Bunbury Banter Theatre Company; Lighting Designer for the butoh dance performance *Project Godie* for Surface Area Dance Theatre Company; and Lighting Designer for *The Gruffalo, the Witch and the Warthog* with Julia Donaldson.

Selina Thompson Ltd

Selina Thompson Ltd is an interdisciplinary company making work that is urgent, playful and intimate. Since 2012 we've made work for pubs, clubs, hairdressers, shopping centres, galleries and theatres.

In 2016, Selina retraced the Transatlantic Slave Triangle by cargo ship and made **salt.** following a six-week attachment at the National Theatre Studio. Since then, the play has been presented in Melbourne, Sao Paulo, Canada, the US and as part of the British Council Showcase during a sell-out run at the Edinburgh Fringe Festival.

In 2017, we were commissioned by 1418NOW as part of *Represent* to deliver a new major gallery piece at the Arnolfini, Bristol, in response to one hundred years since some women got the vote.

For the next five years we will be working with groups of teenage girls all over the world for 'The Missy Elliott Project', making works in performance, virtual reality and online in response to their lives and experiences.

Since 2013, our live work has reached over 12,000 people.

'Thompson is so personable you could eat her up'
Lyn Garden, *The Guardian*

'A force of nature' – *The Stage*

'An inspiration – *The Independent*

Featured in *The Stage* 100 Most Influential Leaders 2018

Named in the Top Ten Black British Women Killing it in their Field' – *Buzzfeed*

Tour Dates 2018

2–3 October   LEEDS PLAYHOUSE

4–5 October   OXFORD PLAYHOUSE

15–16 October   BIRMINGHAM REPERTORY THEATRE

25–27 October   HOME, MANCHESTER

Acknowledgements

salt. was a community undertaking, and as such I would like to thank:

Emma Beverley: my producer, and partner in crime; Ria Hartley, Misri Day, Jo Bannon and Hannah Silva for that first week in Falmouth, and Lubaina Himid for the time I spent at the Making Histories Visible Archive, the two hundred people that supported our kickstarter, the core of the project – and I want to thank the countless people that shared it and forwarded it, and kept it in people's line of sight, Erica Packington who has been the project's patron throughout, the Arts Council, the British Council, Mayfest, Hayley Reid, Charlotte Cooper, all the people – too many to name – that we connected with in Jamaica and Ghana.

I'd like to thank Xana, Minette and Nyima, Matt who did the massages in Bristol, and (the angel) Gabe who did the massages in Edinburgh, Clare Duffy, Nadia Fall, and the Dark Room Team, everybody involved in Yorkshire Festival, and especially the class of eight-year-olds that came and reviewed that version of the show .

I'd like to thank Maddy Costa and Season Butler, Bryony Kimmings, Marcia X and my board – Scottee, Martin Bailey, Rebecca Joy Novell, Akwugo Emejulu, Clare Clarkson and Priya Jethwa, Hannah Pool and everybody at Africa Utopia and the Southbank Centre; the Attenborough Centre, especially Laura Mc Dermott; the team at Northern Stage with a special shout out to their Edinburgh 2017 tech team and volunteers, Sharon and PR team, because I am grumpy and I hate PR, Deb and Jen, Mel Purdie, Sarah Manning, Claire Clarke, Kat Radreva, Cassie Mitchell, Tim and Tanuja, Louise, and Dawn, for taking the work to the next level.

I want to thank my artist peers, especially Yolanda, Rachael, Paula, Mara, Annie, Adura, Apphia, Julene, Tessa, Krishna, Joyce, Bridget, Sue and Chris.

And to the people I text pretty much every day – Emily, Dorrit, Travers, Issy, Candice, Vic, Toni, Demi, Louisa and Wendy.

And finally, a big thank you to my mum, my dad and my sister, Naomi.

But I want to especially thank the POC audiences, specifically the Black audiences

Who have sat in those rooms in the minority

And negotiated an audience that is often negotiating things
a lifetime of whiteness has told them that they don't have to
negotiate in that space –

And sometimes they decide that they would rather not.

So it means the space of coming to that show is often not a safe
one for you. I see that, and I appreciate it, and I love you for it,
fiercely.

I am a lot to carry! And y'all do.

salt.

Selina Thompson is an artist and performer whose work has been shown and praised internationally. Her practice is primarily intimate, political and participatory with a strong emphasis on public engagement that leads to joyous, highly visual work that seeks to connect with those often marginalised by the arts. Her work is focused on the politics of identity, and how this defines our bodies, lives and environments. She has made work for pubs, cafés, hairdressers, toilets and sometimes galleries and theatres, including Spill Festival of Performance, the National Theatre Studio, Birmingham REP, East Street Arts and the West Yorkshire Playhouse. as well as theatres in Europe, Brazil, Canada, the US and Australia.

SELINA THOMPSON

salt.

FABER & FABER

First published in 2018
by Faber and Faber Limited
74–77 Great Russell Street
London WC1B 3DA

Typeset by Country Setting, Kingsdown, Kent CT14 8ES
Printed and bound in the UK by CPI Group (UK) Ltd, Croydon CR0 4YY

A CIP record for this book
is available from the British Library

ISBN 978-0-571-35226-5

FSC
www.fsc.org
MIX
Paper from
responsible sources
FSC® C013604

2 4 6 8 10 9 7 5 3 1

A Small Note

I try to be very quiet around **salt.** A little bit, I try to recede from the attention that it garnered, and the praise, I think because . . . because even if everybody had hated it, I would have done it anyway. I had hit an impasse, in my very bones, in the very delicate fragments that make up my soul, and I did the journey that made this work to bring the fragments back together. But even here, I am saying what is already in the text.

Everything I have to say about the work, you hold in your hands.

So I pass the task of introducing the work to Alexandrina Helmsley, an artist I love, admire and respect, who saw this show in Edinburgh, and truly saw me.

I dedicate this work to Isabella Douglas, my mother's mother, my wonderful Nanny, who told me that she would be there waiting for me when I returned, and who sent me to sea with the shelter of her love around me.

SELINA THOMPSON

Introduction

Watching, watching, watching as Selina Thompson roots herself and starts unfolding her insides. Hers is a work of exhuming the dead. **salt.** traces their ghostly forms so that we might honour their meticulous, industrial decimation. In her hands, there are tools: a very big hammer, a pestle, a mic. She is pounding. Pounding salt and pounding her heart. These two masses linked; both formed over time and broken over time.

The first time Selina used her passport was to undertake a task too great for her, too brutal to hold. But hold it her body does. She is holding the chain linking white colonial patriarchy, along to capitalism and down to her own terror on board a freight ship that is sailing the Atlantic Slave Trade route. Through all this, she pounds salt. The ocean, the bodies of slaves, the flinches of white liberal people confronted by racism, are all 'swept up and scattered' as hammer hits rock. And still Selina stands whole.

We are watching courage. The raw type. The courage that catches off guard. The courage that is not a choice but accompanies an imperative calling. A calling that draws Selina – like many who are part of the African diaspora – to find out and grieve both the documented presences and eroded absences of the slave trade.

Selina tells the racist tale that a racist teacher told her grandmother. It is a story about how black people came to exist. There were two people. One day they were both soiled with dirt. One was hard-working and went to wash away their stains in the sea. They became white. The other was lazy and only washed their palms and soles of their feet. They became black.

Of course, dirty stains are not on the bodies of black people but in the waters soiled by the dirt of others' hands and minds. White British slave traders stained the deceptively clear waters, and yet a black child hears her origin perversely twisted. History mishandles history.

It is a history that although effortfully uncovered by many, can still be subjected to tidal denials that result in it feeling frustratingly ungraspable. In the UK today, there are only optional modules within the national curriculum where pupils from the African diaspora may learn of their traumas and their belonging. The ongoing impacts of slavery remain unfathomable; they are formless down to the depths of the ocean, right down to the watery, sub-atomic reckonings with grief.

Later, Selina speaks of something – will, hands, strength, current – bringing her out of this water and back into form. She finds language for the unspeakable. Through salty tears that prickle – having learnt as a teenager that it is not safe to cry about slavery in a majority white space – I see her.

ALEXANDRINA HELMSLEY

Choreographer, performer and writer, Alexandrina believes in dance and the body as a site for expressing felt and embodied politics. She is interested in liminal spaces, connectivity, fracturing, displacement and emotionality.

salt. was first performed at the Southbank Centre, London, in July 2017. It was restaged in many venues including the Edinburgh Festival in 2017, and commenced a national tour at Leeds Playhouse on 1 October 2018. The cast was as follows:

The Woman Selina Thompson

Directed by Dawn Walton
Designed by Katherina Radeva
Lighting Design by Cassie Mitchell
    Relights by Louise Gregory
Sound Design by Tanuja Amarasuriya
Music composed by Sleepdogs
Dramaturgical support from Maddy Costa
    and Season Butler
Produced by Emma Beverley
Production Managed by Louise Gregory

salt.

Before the Journey

There is an ocean: a blue, velvet drape that hangs from ceiling to floor upstage left.

There is a triangle: three fluorescent strip-lights hanging from the ceiling, or attached to the back wall.

There is a wake: a microphone on a stand and a rotting funeral wreath.

There is a broom: on the very periphery, almost offstage, a simple, wooden broom with strong bristles – a wide broom is best.

There is an island: upstage right there is a high, wooden chair, surrounded by tall tropical houseplants

There is an altar: a narrow table made of natural, unvarnished wood, with one additional shelf set just upstage from centre.

There is a rock: beneath the workstation is a large, heavy chunk of rock salt. The rock should be naturally formed. We used pink, Himalayan rock salt.

There is a sledgehammer: on the shelf below the workstation, accompanied by safety goggles and white safety gloves.

There are libations: a long-necked bottle atop the altar with rosemary suspended in the water that is inside it, a glass of water, incense and a burner, and a pestle and mortar that contains some finely ground rock salt.

The space is ready for work.

Everything the Woman needs to tell the story is on stage with her.

All materials are natural. Wood. Water. Salt. Plants. Glass. Simple, clean.

There is only one performer. The Woman. She is standing or siting behind this table, waiting. The incense burns to ready her for the work to come.

The space has been spiritually cleansed, and is ready for the spirit work that is to take place.

In the audience there is a row of safety goggles on the seats of the first few rows.

As people enter, the Woman is listening to music that brings her strength and calm. The lights dim and just before the show starts:

The Woman During this show, I'll be working with a sledgehammer and safety goggles. The rule is, that when I am wearing mine, you also need to be wearing yours.

There is a beat. We begin.

I am twenty-eight.
I am Black.
I am a woman.

I grew up in Birmingham which is where all my family live.

I am second generation and third.
By which I mean

I'm adopted. Both my birth parents, my mother and father, were Rastafarians from Jamaica, who moved to the UK when they were thirteen.

The parents who adopted me, my mum and dad, were both born here, and their parents were from Jamaica and Montserrat.

And we are all descended from enslaved people.

On a form, I tick 'Black British'.

If you ask me where I'm from I'll say Birmingham.

If you ask me where I'm really from, I'll think 'Suck your mom!' but I'll say, 'My parents were born here.'

And if you ask me where my grandparents are from, in my head I'll flip over a table; but out loud, I'll say 'Jamaica'.

On the twelfth of February 2016 I got on a cargo ship in Antwerp in Belgium, and sailed from there to Tema in Ghana. It took three weeks. I spent a week in Ghana, along the coast, before flying to Kingston in Jamaica, via Dubai and New York. This took forty hours. I then spent two and half weeks in Jamaica living in Bull Bay near Kingston before spending Easter weekend on Treasure Beach. After this I flew to Wilmington in North Carolina via Atlanta, in Georgia, where I got on another freighter that sailed across the Atlantic and took me to Antwerp.

I arrived in Birmingham, UK, on the twelfth of April, and stood with my mum and dad in their kitchen, holding hands. Then my mum went to work at Dorothy Perkins, and my dad made himself a sandwich before going to sign on.

I was twenty-five, and it was the first time I had used my adult passport.

A beat.

When I try to remember it, it is a dream.
I am here to tell you a story of the diaspora.
A story of people swept up and scattered across the world.

She pours the libation.
She takes a moment.

The Woman places the rock salt in place, ready for
smashing.
  It is too heavy for her to lift.
  She gets into a position for storytelling.

The Woman We are sat together, my nan and I, and she
turns to me and tells me a story I have always known,
and never placed, she turns to me and she says:

'I was the only black girl in my school – it was a
different time then. And I was aware of it, but I didn't
think of it.

'One day, a girl put her hand up, and she asked why
black people were black, and white people were white,
and why black people weren't completely black.

'And the teacher turned to her and said that "There used
to be only two humans in the world, and one day, they
both went somewhere that they shouldn't have gone, and
when they came back, they were dirty, stained by the
dirt.

'So they turned to God, and they said,

'"What can we do to be clean again?"

'And God said,

'"If you go down to the sea in the morning before the
tide goes out, you can wash the stain off yourselves."

'So the two humans went to sleep, with the intent the
next day to wash themselves clean.

'Now, one human was good and hard-working, so they
woke up easily – went down to the sea, and washed

themselves clean, and stood in the sun, sparkling and white.

'The other human was lazy and forgetful – they overslept – so by the time that they arrived at the ocean, the tide was leaving. They only had enough time to put the bottoms of their feet and the palms of their hands in the water. So that was the only part of them that was washed off. They remained stained.'

That's what she said, the teacher. That's what she said, to my grandmother, as a child.

Breaking the Burden Open

The Woman puts on her safety goggles, and safety gloves, and intimates that the audience members that have them should do the same.
She breaks open the salt rock, she smashes at Europe.

The First Point: Europe

The Woman takes off her gloves and safety goggles,
places them and sledgehammer back on the work
station.
   She stands, beneath the glare of Europe, embodying
its arrogance.

The Woman We are in Europe, it is where I have always
lived,

in Europe,
wealthy, wealthy Europe

And let me say now, clearly
Explicitly,
with no risk of being misunderstood

Europe is awash in blood. Every penny of wealth, each
brick of each intimidating building, the pavement slabs
of quiet city streets and the soil beneath rolling green
hillside is built on suffering, massacre, death. It is, and
should be, a cursed continent.

And I have always lived here.
Europe

in the UK specifically
and on this occasion
in Scotland,
in Edinburgh,
in an off-licence
gazing
at my phone.

It is 2014.
Time accumulates
And to me that means

I go and see a show at the Edinburgh Festival. One, two, three, four shows where white men shout about their pain, where race is an afterthought.

One show, in particular, in making a point about psychology, stages the words of a white supremacist with no thought for anyone of colour in the room and

Every word feels like it has torn off my skin but
I'm living with the person that made it.
And I was the only black person in the room, my dark skin made luminous.

So I call my nan, cry out to her, and she says 'But this is what white people are like, you know this, you've known this, calm down, get back in there, you are there to work.' And she is right, and I do know this. So I get back in there. Two halves of who I am, a body that works, educated in white institutions, and a body that feels, nurtured in black homes, smash together like tectonic plates and as they do something in me –

2014:
Ferguson in August,
Protests about the staging of a human zoo in London in September,
The shooting of twelve-year-old Tamir Rice in November,
No indictment for the murder of Eric Garner in December.
I begin to read and read and read and I look around and I see and something in me –.

I am growing accustomed to a timeline, an endless feed of black pain, black rage and black people having to assert that black lives matter because black death is normal, the aberration, the deviation from the norm is refusing that. I am filling with this pain and rage and death, can't see, can't think, can't breathe and something in me –

Once I begin to see this I can't stop seeing it, it repeats itself in art, in who we fall in love with, places itself, in what we eat and dance to and who we spend our time with, repeating and repeating and something in me –

Jumping back and forth through time.
2011:
A child in a café in Brighton sits, stares and stares at me, I keep eating
Europe pushes against me, I push back.
2013:
I date a man darker than me, in Leeds, we walk down the street and people stare, we keep walking
Europe pushes against me, I push back.
2006:
A man in a gallery in London jabs my shoulder and asks where stereotypes of absent black fathers come from.
I keep quiet
Europe pushes against me, I push back.
2008:
A child cries in my arms in Birmingham because a friend's parent 'Don't want no black girl round her house', I keep hugging her
Europe pushes against me, I push back.
2012:
My entrance silences an entire pub in a small village in North Yorkshire, I keep heading towards the bar
Europe pushes against me, I push back.
2014:
'Look, Mummy, a nigger' in Bristol, I keep going
Europe pushes against me.

Race imposed onto the skin
And something in me –

I am a walking wound for a year, a raw nerve left
exposed. All of the poison of the world is seeping into
me, adrenaline in my body, depression without end.
Nothing is big enough.

It is time travel. Sometimes I stand at the bus stop, and
I think about the violence that is in my ancestry, the
violence embedded in our lives and the world shimmers
and then melts away and all that is left is suffering.
Nothing is OK and there is no way it can be OK. It's like
a lens, the feeling, it clicks into place distorting everything,
and exposing it for what it really is.

My time travel doesn't land anywhere. Once the lens
clicked into place I couldn't make it go away and I don't
want to. I choose to not move on. I refuse to get over
what is not yet over, the thought makes me want to
vomit but something in me –

I watch a film, and a black woman's voice is heard in the
loneliness of space, over and over again, 'It's after the
end of the world don't you know that yet?' and I
reposition the world, I think about how the world looks
if slavery and colonialism were the end of it, and we are
living post apocalypse now, or living in an ever-recurring
apocalypse, spinning back and repeating itself. I try to
unpick the magnitude of this grief that exists in a world
with pubs and the post office and aroma diffusers from
Muji also in it and something in me –

What is it to turn away from Europe when it took so
many people resisting and making sacrifices and surviving
to bring you there? How do you negotiate that gift, how
do you grieve? I am one foot in and one foot out,
complicit and something in me –

A friend draws the triangle for me, of Europe, Africa, Caribbean. I want to go to the middle of the ocean not to drown but to be alone, apart, and maybe my chest will fill with enough water for it to . . .
We're sat at a conference, in the shadow of Stuart Hall, and my friend tells me to go to sea. To go to sea and write this.
And so I go, with the presence of an audience around me, as cloying as it is comforting, and something in me –

I tell my mother and she is terrified, a deep fear, from the darkest most afraid parts of herself, she says: 'You won't just be a woman travelling alone, you'll be a Black Woman travelling alone in those countries and if something happens to you, no one will care, no one will look after you.'

And I have no response.

But the decision to go is not one she can interfere with. I am carrying a weight I can't bear much longer

I have to find a way to live or some peace, something in me –

I do not go alone. I bring with me a filmmaker, who I will not name, another child of the diaspora, another sibling, another artist to plunge into this feeling with me, to do what artists do and reflect and create, imagine new ways of living. Having those two textures – film and performance – invigorates me, gives the project potential for new depth. I do not think about the risk this might put them at, and in not naming them now, and not seeking to tell their story on her behalf, I'm trying not to repeat that harm. But we set out together,

Britain, Germany, Belgium

each with their own history.

Before we get on the ship, we sign a contract.
One: the cargo comes first and takes precedence over everything else

And

Two: at sea, the Master's word is law.

I sign.

The Master –

blonde curly hair, bright blue eyes, and the sort of infantile, malice-laced bounce that I associate with men like Boris Johnson

Says that he doesn't mind having women there, as a diversion, had he known what our work was about, he would never have agreed to our presence on board. That he doesn't want any trouble. That his ship is not a slave ship.

I explain that we are not making a project about him or his ship, that we want only to film the sea itself, to document our experience,

He tells us that our tickets will be released only if we promise not to film.

Europe pushes against me
everything in me says 'no',

But I relent.

And we are leaving Europe

Or at least we thought we were

But the ship sails under an Italian flag, and even as we leave this point in the triangle, something in me –

The First Side: the Hold

We are at sea. We are moving through the triangle.

WE REMEMBER THE DEAD
AND MAKE THE SEA

The Woman contemplates the Salt.

The Woman Tears and sweat
stinging and dissolving
healing
forming crystals
the residue of great rocks being
ground down across time.

> *The Woman begins to arrange the Salt. She lines nine
> chunks out across the stage, in order of size.*
> *The biggest is stage left, and the smallest at stage
> right.*

Time accumulates.
You are at sea with me and it is February.

There are twenty-seven of us

And we are sailing to Ghana, via Benin, Nigeria, the
Ivory Coast, Senegal.

Carrying cars and marble.
The six white officers speak Italian.
The nineteen Asian crew members speak Filipino.
So the two Black women sit in silence
There is no phone reception, no internet.

We eat with the officers.
And we notice that the word 'nigger' keeps coming up
at dinner.
I try to tell myself that maybe it is an Italian seafaring
word.
I hear the master say 'Chinaman'.
I give up.

The Master is a big man. He will look in my face at
dinner as he refers to Africans as niggers as loudly as
I am speaking to you now.

He will stand outside my door and say it.

One afternoon I watch the film *Sankofa* which ends with
an uprising in which all the enslaved massacre their
oppressors.

Later when I sit at dinner, my rage buzzes around the
table. I remember why I am here, and the history that
holds me. I cause a tremor of panic to vibrate across the
shiny white tableware and so the next day, he makes a
point of coming to talk to me

And it's fine to begin with

But he can't help himself, and so he tells me his thoughts
on Africa.

He tells me that the people are feral children,

He tells me that the continent will never progress,

He tells me to be wary of Africans,

Who, he tells me, will hate me worst of all,

He finishes up by telling me that racism is ancient history.

He knows I will say nothing. It is cartoon racism,
impolite, brutish racism, not the smooth slick polite
confused racism of my liberal friends

The shock it creates feels like blow to the skull.

I give up.

She gives up.

He has stopped us from filming, and in doing so, he takes a massive chunk of my project away from me, and a creative outlet away from my collaborator.

He took the three grand that we paid him, and did everything he could to crush our work, and to crush us. I am left with the shame of not having been able to stop him. It is so bad that when we arrive on dry land, my filmmaker and I decide that she can go home. We have lost a month's worth of footage, and have to find a new way out of no way.

But this will come later.

Right now, we are still on board.

Not allowed on the deck, we have no windows in our cabins. no sunlight. A paranoia about stowaways pervades every port, so when we are in dock, the doors of the ship are locked with us inside. No fresh air.

I stop eating, stop turning up for the meals – each three courses long, mountains of pasta, slabs of meat, sour oranges and soft apples. Pizza on Saturdays, ice cream on Sundays. Stodgy and heavy with eight-hour gaps between them.

My period sits thickly inside my body, and I curl into the corner of my bed and make myself as small as I can, and sometimes, if it is too much, and the writing does not help, I claw at my chest.

And sometimes at night I listen to 'Hotline Bling' and imagine the pinks and blues of the video as I fall asleep.

Sometimes at night AC/DC and Led Zeppelin is played by the Master at the bottom of the corridor loud enough to make my room shake.

Sometimes at night there is no music and the dead come up through the ship for me.

> *The Woman goes and gathers some of the smaller fragments of rock that broke off when she first began to hit at Europe.*
> *She takes it to the pestle and mortar, and uses it to help her tell the next part of her story.*

The Hold: Womb, Tomb, Bowel

Bed on a ship in a room no worse than the average Travelodge – two single beds, a small desk, a little shower room. Wipe-clean floor, fluorescent safety lights and no windows.

I sit at the desk, and I open *Lose Your Mother* by Saidiya Hartman. I feel them around me, the people whose words I read at sea. Saidiya across the desk, Audre Lorde to my right, Marlon James furiously scribbling away to my left and bell hooks with her hands in the small of my back.

Saidiya writes:

'All the terrible details of the slave trade thundered in my head . . . nothing helped.'

I turn the page, and together we fill our minds and bodies with this anguish:

asphyxiations and decapitations and drowning, suffocation and flesh boiled in sugar cane, bodies blown up with gunpowder, hanged, burned at the stake, bodies left to putrefy, pecked at by vultures, devoured alive by fire

ants, roasted on pikes. The fodder of the horror films
I never have the stomach to watch vibrating in my
throat, echoing through our DNA and choking us both.

But above all, the trail of bleached bones stretching out
across the middle passage, beneath my feet, added to
every single day

and the final violence, of those that would forget it
happened, that would ignore how it shaped the world.

At sea
Passing over so much death
Floating through it.

I don't think the sea wants us here
It is impossible to pay our respects.

> *The Woman returns to her safety goggles and safety
> gloves, and picks up the sledgehammer. The next part
> of the ritual is coming.*

On board, in our floating portion of Europe things are
circling round and repeating themselves.

WE NAME THE BURDENS

The Woman picks up her sledgehammer.
   *She performs a new nursery rhyme, accompanied by
rhythmic smashing with a sledgehammer.*
   *Each chunk of rock represents a character or force on
the ship. They are smashed at every time they are
referenced.*
   *By the end, the rocks representing the two Black folk
are finely ground dust, almost invisible. The final rock
remains pretty much intact.*

The Woman Me
And the artist

Another Black artist
We are stood eye to eye
Or in rooms where we cry.
I'm shouting at them
And they're shouting at me
And we're still at sea in the morning

This is the Crew
The Filipino crew
Silenced, suspicious, they just don't speak
There's no solidarity for the artist
I'm shouting at them
And they're shouting at me
And we're still at sea in the morning.

These are the Officers,
White,
Italian,
Officers
Calling us niggers, lurking about
They alienate the crew
And terrorise the artists
I'm shouting at them
And they're shouting at me
And we're still at sea in the morning.

This is the Master
I despise calling him Master
His control is held by intimidation and aggression
He bullies the officers
They alienate the crew
And terrorise the artists
Shouting at them
And they're shouting at me
And we're still at sea in the morning.

This is the Union
A corrupted union

They campaign ineffectively so rights are abused
This grinds down the master
He bullies the officers
They alienate the crew
And terrorise the artists
Shouting at them
And they're shouting at me
And we're still at sea in the morning.

This is the Company
A capitalist company
Pays its workers a pittance, works them seven days a week
They corrupt the union
That grinds down the master
He bullies the officers
They alienate the crew
And terrorise the artists
Shouting at them
And they're shouting at me
And we're still at sea in the morning.

These are the States
European
States
Feeding off 'the other' to stay in control
That pressure the company
That corrupts the union
That grinds down the master
He bullies the officers
They alienate the crew
And terrorise the artists
Shouting at them
And they're shouting at me
And we're still at sea in the morning.

And this is imperialism and racism and capitalism and
God knows what else

Built on violence
Maintained by it too
It decides who matters and who will die
It shapes the states
That pressure the company
That corrupts the union
That grinds down the master
He bullies the officers
They alienate the crew
And terrorise the artists
Shouting at them
And they're shouting at me
And we're still at sea in the –

The ship grinds to a halt.

I am trying to remember, always that all are suffering, all carry their burden, all are bound up in each other. Still. Sometimes, when I am alone, I think back to being on that ship, I think that I should have spat in that man's face before I reached dry land.

The Woman places her sledgehammer, safety gloves and safety goggles back in place.

THE FIRST GATEKEEPER

There is a pause.
A golden moment, where the Woman and audience ground themselves and connect.
The Woman goes and gets the broom, and as she tells the story, takes us out of Europe.

The Woman I finally get the chance to call my dad. He picks up the phone and says,

'Tell me what you've been doing then!' he says.

The Woman's dad is a Brummie, and he has Jamaican parents.

So I tell him the story of my last day on the ship, I say, 'As you can imagine I was pretty desperate to get off this stupid boat, so come six a.m. I was packed, bag on back, ready to go, come let's do this.

'And the Master said it would be another couple of hours.

'So I'm sort of sitting, staring into the void that is my doorway when out of nowhere, three teenage Ghanaian girls – one with braids, one with a relaxed bob, one with a very short afro, walked past my bedroom door. They looked at me. I looked at them. "Hello," they say. "Hi!" I squeal, too loud, too loud. They keep going.

'Two hours go past. The Master says, another two hours.

'So I'm back staring into the void/doorway and they emerge again, walking in the other direction – braids, straight bob, afro – and this time they step over the threshold! They say, "Where did you come from?" and I say, "I'm from England," and they say, "What?!" and I ay, "What?!" and then they keep going.

'Two hours go past. I decide I have had enough, I am getting off this ship, so I go to find the Master.

'And he's not there but they are, this time in high-vis jackets, braids, straight bob, afro and I say, "Where did you come from?" and they say, "We're here on work experience!" and I say, "Of course you are," and they laugh, and so I shake their hands, instead of the Master's, and their giggling and energy takes me off the ship and into Tema, into Ghana.'

And my dad says,

'Did anybody else see these three teenage Ghanaian girls?'

I say, 'No.'

He says, 'Are you making this up?'

I say, 'No!'

And he says, 'Hmmm.'

The Second Point: Africa

The Woman approaches the microphone and the wreath. She delivers a eulogy.

The Woman To be a descendant of slaves visiting Ghana as a site of ancestry is to try to go somewhere that doesn't exist to look for somebody no one has heard of.

The person who expresses this most clearly is probably Saidiya Hartman, and her writing is what shapes my time in Ghana.

I cannot really tell you much about Ghana. I was there ten days, with the lens of the transatlantic slave trade over my eyes, pinning me to a mattress most days. To go with that lens is to go without truly seeing.

This lens is most apparent when I visit a town on the coast called Elmina, a town famous for a castle that stands on its coastline. This castle, bleached white by the sun, and set against a gorgeous tableau of palm trees and blue sea, was the place where people went through the Door of No Return, and out into the Middle Passage to become slaves. It was the hold before the hold. And now, it is where someone like me goes to grieve. Or make art. Or, as the guestbook told me, be surprised by the presence of castles in Africa.

In *Lose your Mother*, Hartman goes to Elmina fifty times – over fifty times, she says. She is looking to satisfy her grief. But when she goes there, she can't find anything. It's empty for her. Hartman despairs, because the slaves she has gone to grieve left long ago. She goes looking for so much and finds it empty.

When I go it's full. Of heat, of humidity, of smell, of pressure. It's like being inside a migraine.

It takes three hours to get there and I beg to leave after an hour.

The women's dungeons reek, we stand in a courtyard where women would have stood, looking up to where the governor would have selected a woman from. The reality of what being selected would have meant, lingers in the air. We go on with the tour.

There is a bit when our tour guide,

who keeps trying to get us to buy a book and DVD,

locks us in the room where those that rebelled were left to starve. We stand in there, in the dark, silently screaming. We try not to run out of the room too quickly when he opens the door.

In each room we find rotting wreaths that have been left, too late, surrounded by flies.

Elmina heaves, and then I am home, scraping grit and dust and sweat and tears off my body, desperately waiting for a period that just won't come.

Time accumulates.

The day that we go to visit Elmina also happens to be the day of my nan's funeral. She is my first big death, the ally of my teenage years, the voice always telling me to rest. She died suddenly, my first day on the ship.

I sit on my grief for her. Hoard it up, store it, I'm greedy with it. I cannot believe I am going to miss my nan's funeral, or that I have left my family grieving. So I hold my grief. I'm stood in Elmina, mourning strangers that it feels impossible to mourn, while all my family are together in Birmingham mourning one of the people I loved most.

I'm holding off until we get to her grave. In my head I'll
get to where she's buried – I'll see it and my grief will be
satisfied. That's going to be the place.

So on my first Sunday back my parents drive me there.
They take me to where she is, but there's nothing there.
She's been buried beside my grandad – so I am at a grave
that I have already visited. The double tombstone is yet
to be engraved, so nothing marks it. The double grave
was not dug properly, so a small mound is there where
the pot of her ashes has been buried. Rotting wreaths
surrounded by flies, because I am here too late. Nanny is
not there. There is nothing here. I am Saidiya in Elmina.
It's all wrong.

> *The eulogy finishes, and the Woman returns to the
> pestle and mortar, and pours a salt libation as she
> finishes her time in Ghana.*

What should a site of mourning for the enslaved look
like?
What might hold the long, long memory?
What would be both a covenant to never let such things
happen again
And a refusal to forget?

THE SECOND GATEKEEPER

A second golden moment.

The Woman Accra Airport. I call my dad.

'Tell me what you've been doing then!'

'It was Independence Day, we went to the parade!
There was a judo display
And women balancing eggs on their heads.
We went with Obed, who is caring for us, taking us

37

around. He gets us good seats in Independence Square. He's quite fit.

'It is this euphoric jubilant day, and as we celebrate together, Obed asks us if we have Independence Day in England and I laugh, really long and really loud from my belly. "No!" I exclaim. The English are who everybody got freedom from!" And Obed and I are in hysterics –'

'Were you flirting with that Ghanaian boy?'

'No, Daddy!'

'Was there really judo at the Ghanaian Independence Day parade?'

'YES! And policewomen doing tricks on motorcycles.'

'Hmmm.'

The Second Side: an Airport

As the Woman tries to make her way to Jamaica, she is distracted, and finds herself in a place of great discomfort. She gets trapped for a time, at the border.

The Woman I have never travelled alone before; and this is the beginning of me developing something of a taste for it, as my British passport lets me scuttle lightly around the world –

Accra
Dubai
New York
Kingston
Georgia
North Carolina.

And later

Hong Kong
Macau
The Netherlands
Texas
and
Spain.

It is the great privilege of a second-slash-third generation child of the diaspora. It troubles and muddles. It reveals the limits of solidarity.

But as this shiny red book demands that other countries –

'Let me pass freely without let or hindrance, afforded assistance and protection as might be necessary'

– I become increasingly aware of myself carrying extra
baggage

I'm trying to locate it on my body

Sometimes it seems to be in my hair
Because it doesn't matter what country I'm in
If it's wrapped or out
Plaited beneath a hat
Twisted ready for flying

It needs excavating.

Sometimes I think it is somewhere in my fat
A squeeze here
Some fingers down a fat fold there
It needs excavating.

Perhaps it's at the top of my legs
The man at JFK definitely seems to think so.

It can't be too big
The airport attendant in Jamaica only noticed it when
she saw the West African visas in my passport.

I would go so far as to say it's invisible,
Because in Hong Kong, apropos of nothing I was
screened for disease not once, not twice, but five times
on arrival as everybody else on my flight walked past me

It needs excavating.

I join a host of Black women
Detained in rooms
Told to remove their wigs
Removed from first class
Asked to pull down their trousers to prove they're
wearing underwear
Dragged off planes

As others are dragged on in the dead of the night

This extra baggage we can't quite shift, keeping us in
and locking us out
But I still get on the plane –

And in a few months' time, I will walk, eyes carefully
averted, past the family, read as Muslim, having the
contents of their lives spread across tables by invasive
hands.

Still, I get on the plane –

I carefully,
diligently
play my role
perform
the well-behaved
citizen
in the airport

No drugs here
I won't be any trouble.

I get on the plane –

Because these experiences resonate with but pale in
comparison to

Bodies washing up from the Mediterranean Sea
A contemporary grave, not historic
Packed together on leaking boats and ranked top to
bottom by shade
Because residual trauma I inherit
Is not the same as trauma experienced and embodied
Resonant
A wound
Not the same.

But it takes distance to see this.

Right now I'm tired and yearning for the comfort of home, for my mum and dad for a nan who has moved forward into the next life

So as we fly over the grave, I watch *Desmond's* –

A clip of Desmond's *plays, projected onto the ocean. Shirley and Porkpie discuss the difficulties of Desmond's desire to end his days in Guyana after he and his wife have spent more than thirty years in the UK.*

The Third Point: Jamaica

The Woman stands in front of Jamaica.

The Woman Time accumulates.

It is March and I am in Jamaica.

Land of my mothers and fathers, and their mothers and fathers – except for one, who came from Montserrat. Land of my birth parents. Land of wood and water. Land of my blood. The island we left. Hung on the wall, embroidered in glitter thread. The outline at the bottom of the tray hung up in the kitchen, engraved into the shiny mahogany ashtray that no one puts their ash into.

She sits at the top of a mountain.

It is

Paradise.

Fecundity defines Jamaica, it is everywhere, life, and I rest: fecundity, fertility, bursting and exploding tiny pale white green butterflies surrounding bright pink and orange flowers, my appetite coming back, a tugging of the womb out of sluggishness, pressure lifting, my legs are scarlet, shiny, sticky . . . period. At last.

It's Easter, so I eat buns, eat cheese, eat fish, and sleep. Near to where I stay a suitcase full of kittens, a puppy sleeping on top of his father, yard dogs, goats wandering down from the mountains every day, chickens and cockerels and bulls and cows, and then fruit pushing out of buds everywhere – ackee and apples and breadfruit and mangoes and guava and pimento and oranges,

43

everywhere you look is full of life: mongooses! Tiny boys chasing crabs down the beach as they run away from the sea that is edging further and further towards us, and I rest.

The next day, exploring Kingston, the taxi driver told me while we drove to Devon House, built by Jamaica's first black millionaire, that the governor's wife hated it so much – said it was an affront – that they built a whole new road so that she wouldn't have to drive past a black man's wealth – 'Lady Musgrave Road? More like Racist White Lady Lane,' the driver says. And I rest.

Looking at mongooses, here because they were bought by slave-owners to kill rats

Looking at bamboo planted to stop the skin of white women going dark in the sun

Looking at private beaches where Jamaicans can't go

Looking at those children playing with a kite that is a wire hanger and a plastic bag, they are so black against the brightness of the sun on this black beach that no tourists come to because they wish it was white so much so that I am told a rumour, that resorts used to buy white sand from the Sahara to cover the black sand, forgetting that the very nature of sand is to wash away and reveal –

Looking at white tourists coming to enact a dynamic in which they are the master and black people smile and serve happily and I am somewhere between; not giving my email address to the woman that wants help with a visa and silently listening to the white woman at our resort saying, 'I'm vulnerable here, as a white woman, so vulnerable to the men.'

Looking, looking, looking and wondering about my gaze, forged in Europe.

I am lonely.

But here, I can look for peace. And there are quiet times, when I sit in silence and stare at the sea with a man who reminds me of my dad or look out over the mountains, with a woman who could be an older sister. I still dream about Jamaica. Think often of how to go back.

In Jamaica, I skype my dad a lot.

I am too tired to tell him what I've been doing, so instead, he tells me about what he would have been doing.

'Did I ever tell you about the pineapple?'

I say, tell me now.

'So my first day in Jamaica, when I was eight, your Grandad Mac gave me a pineapple, and told me to share it with my sister. I never ate a pineapple so sweet! You think I shared? Not a bite!

'So the next day, your Grandad Mac gives me a second pineapple, and he says, "You eat every drop of that pineapple." I never tasted something so sour! And no one to share. Not a soul. I learnt from there.'

My mum is giggling in the corner of the screen, in her bonnet and her reading glasses, doing a crossword. They are in bed together, their room in my room in Jamaica, the sea, and the sound of their little electric heater mingled together.

Jamaica and Ghana were always places real, imagined and imaginary for him, as a father, and as a man.

Would you come back, I say? With me? I wish you were here.

He won't go back to Jamaica, he says, because it's not

what it was when he was there as a child. 'I don't know anyone there any more. It's not home.'

In a taxi and here it comes, the question please don't ask me the question

'Do you have family here?'

Biological parents I never knew, a family my mum and dad did not think to introduce me to, so I should be here with people, I have family here but I do not know them because we left, they left.

In Jamaica it's where are you from, where are your family from

In England it will be where are you from, where are you really from

In Ghana it was where are you from, and then a guess of where my people might be from

I think that so much of being a part of the diaspora is seeking home

In places where you can't belong and in people that you can't belong

Time accumulates.

And I am sat beside my nan in hospital, days before she dies, before the voyage. And she tells me about the beauty of Montserrat, puts all the joy of the world in that single word – tells me of sailing at sixteen with three brothers to England – of half the island on one ship with ambition and hope – of the man in the cabin beside her vomiting, and her stealing his food.

Time accumulates.

A film clip begins to fade up on the sheet and the Woman, both in and out of Jamaica. It is from The

Harder They Come, *and shows its protagonist trying to swim from the shore of Jamaica to the ship that will take him away from danger. He wakes on the shore.*

Still in Jamaica, in March. The beach outside my house is black pebbles and rocks and I stand, stand in the sea, and the water comes up to the middle of my ankles and I feel like I am walking on the water, like I am part of the water, like the ocean can command me and I can command it, everywhere I look this foam and me in the middle of it. I could do it. Walk down into the sea and keep walking till I re-emerged at the other side, home. The diaspora heaves with those stories –

If we didn't eat salt, we could fly home,
That we could sing our way home
That the spirits would guide us home
That we knew our way home.

But I'm still in Jamaica and a cargo ship goes across my eyeline

Not yet, not just yet.

The Third Gatekeeper

One last golden moment.

The Woman Time accumulates.

She steps down from the mountain.

Early April and I am stood on the dock.
And my dad says
'Come on then, one last time before you get in the sea.
Tell me what you been up to then?'

Before I could go on the ship, I had to stay over in
North Carolina, in a place called Wilmington, and when
I arrived there was a very, very fat dachshund in the
reception of my hotel. Now, I love a fat animal, but I
was bit worried about it, it kind of sounded like the dog
had asthma. So when I went to sleep that night, having
taken some sedatives, I dreamt about dogs, and when I
wake up, all groggy and sedated, I can still hear one,
barking. And it almost sounds real, so I wonder towards
my door sort of in a bit of a daze –

And when I open the door, the biggest most hench
French bulldog I have ever seen barrels in my room and
begins jumping up on me, on the table in the room,
knocking over lampshades, dragging last night's pizza
out of the box – she barks and barks and gets my
luggage tags and runs out of the room.

When I follow her out into the corridor she is gone. And
I stand there and think, 'Did I dream that?' And a small
woman appears and says, 'I'm so sorry,' she says. 'We
got a French bulldog because they're supposed to be

calm, but there's something wrong with this one.'

'Selina. Did anybody else see this dog or this lady?'

'No, Daddy.'

'Hmmm.'

THE THIRD SIDE: THE ATLANTIC

The Woman prepares the space to deliver another eulogy,
the eulogy of a woman who has jumped into the sea,
using what is on stage. We are underwater.

The Woman And I get onto the final ship.
As I leave, birds dive into the water we leave in our
wake

Where are you from?

No table flipping, no sucking of moms, where are you
from?

All of it, none of it.

But still, I sail, in solitude,
I sail, and do not see land for eleven days
There is no sleep to be had, so on the twelfth night, I rise
up out of bed, intending to make my way out onto the
deck. To taste salt.
My bedroom door is a creamy, rusty white. It towers
above me, it rattles,
Saltwater from the deepest parts of the sea is leaking
down its cracks, the something in me, there before me,
demanding that I answer,
And using every ounce of strength in my body I open the
door.
It is like cracking a seal
And I do not find the corridors to the deck as expected

Instead I see that it opens out onto the waves, that all is air and water and fear and a single step through it will take me down
down to the place where those that did not cross the chasm, who remained suspended in the transformation now reside,
down to those that wait for me
down to be preserved in salt
down to be in all three parts of the triangle, and in the centre of it
down to be where I have always been, down to the only place where I can be
down to my own end of the world
There is no peace to be had, no homes to be found
So I leap
Throw all of me into the abyss
This body plunges into the depths, fathoms deep, and as it falls it changes
Becomes a dead living thing
Is reshaped and reformed by the ocean, into chunks of salt, falling like snow in the sea. White crystals, falling softly to the place with no answers and no secrets freedom from the body at last

And I stay here. Where no one should live. Where only death goes. I stay here, a floating grain of salt, a part of the grave

The Woman drowns, and her body becomes salt.

CLOSING THE RITUAL

But something calls to her.

The Woman But somewhere, out of nothingness, the voice of my nan. The voice of Isabella, calling, calling,

calling my body back into form. Her voice, its love and its command, pulls me back into being, the Salt gives the newly formed body a buoyancy and we are floating together, just above the placeless place. I am holding her hand, and it is so soft. And everything is golden. Sun on our faces, and peace in our hearts. Somehow. Maybe it is just because we are together. And there are other ancestors, just out of sight. It is so safe here. So quiet.

Things are golden.

I turn to her and I say everything the world has grown from and everything the world has grown into makes me want to –

A beat.

And hands are placed on me. Hands in my hands, on the back of my neck, hands on the small of my back, surrounding me and lifting me up, reminding me of all it took to bring me here. Of the need to continue to live. Of how sacred it is to be a descendant of those that were never supposed to survive

And I am lifted up out of the sea

I am not healed. But I do decide to keep living.

A beat. The Woman returns to the space. She is in the room with you.

(*To the audience.*) I'm going to leave this space now. And you will leave too.
And when the last of you has left, you close the space, and we are finished.
But before you go, you will meet me in the foyer with a basket of salt and I ask that you take a piece, wrap it and keep it safe. The salt is not safe for you to eat, but that is not what it is for. To take it is to make a

commitment to live, a commitment to the radical space
of not moving on, and all that it can open.

Salt to heal, salt to remember, salt for your bath, for
your nourishment, and above all for your wounds.

Because I went all that way, it took all that to decide
to live.

This is my monument.

This is my act of remembrance.

This is my grief.

But this is our burden.

Sit with it

Sit with the pain

It won't go away

But I am sitting with you.

And we go on.

Thank you.

The End.